SPORTS
STARTERS

Carve it Snowboarding

Jaime Winters

Crabtree Publishing Company

www.crabtreebooks.com

SPORTS STARTERS

Created by Bobbie Kalman

Author
Jaime Winters

Project coordinator
Kathy Middleton

Editors
Molly Aloian
Rachel Stuckey

Proofreader
Wendy Scavuzzo

Photo research
Melissa McClellan

Design
Tibor Choleva
Melissa McClellan

Production coordinator
Margaret Amy Salter

Prepress technician
Margaret Amy Salter

Print coordinator
Katherine Berti

Consultant
Dustin Heise, BHK, Director of Sport Development-Canada~Snowboard

Illustrations
Leif Peng: page 9

Photographs
Dreamstime.com: © Aleksey Ipatov (titlepage); © Ron Chapple (p 5); © Jaak Kadak (p 10 left); © Jakub Pavlinec (pp 5 (girl), 12 right); © Nikittta (pp 14, 15 top); © Lukasz Kielas (p 16); © Ventura69 (p 21); © Les Palenik (p 22); © Tiziano Casalta (p 24); © Millaus (p 25); © Tiziano Casalta (p 26); © Galina Barskaya (p 31 top right)
Corbis: © Sampics (p 29)
iStockphoto.com: © ParkerDeen (p 4); © mbbirdy (p 6); © walik (p 7); © technotr (p 31 top left); © Michele Galli (p 31)
fotolia: © Denis Babenko (p 10 right); © raven (p 13); Andrey Stratilatov (p 15 bottom)
Shutterstock.com: Noo (front cover); © Marcel Jancovic (toc page); © Jason Merideth (p 11); © iofoto (p 12 left); © AXL (p 17); © Julia Pivovarova (back cover, p 18); © Ipatov (p 19); © Action Photos (p 20); © Nick Stubbs (p 23); © Cappi Thompson (p 27); © Ben Haslam (p 28); © Irina Terentjeva (p 31 left)
Created for Crabtree Publishing by BlueAppleWorks

Library and Archives Canada Cataloguing in Publication

Winters, Jaime
    Carve it snowboarding / Jaime Winters.

(Sports starters)
Includes index.
Issued also in electronic format.
ISBN 978-0-7787-3148-1 (bound).--ISBN 978-0-7787-3159-7 (pbk.)

    1. Snowboarding--Juvenile literature. I. Title.
II. Series: Sports starters (St. Catharines, Ont.)

GV857.S57W558 2012   j796.939   C2012-900881-8

Library of Congress Cataloging-in-Publication Data

Winters, Jaime.
    Carve it snowboarding / Jaime Winters.
        p. cm. -- (Sports starters)
    Includes index.
    ISBN 978-0-7787-3148-1 (reinforced library binding : alk. paper) --
ISBN 978-0-7787-3159-7 (pbk. : alk. paper) -- ISBN 978-1-4271-8846-5
(electronic pdf) -- ISBN 978-1-4271-9749-8 (electronic html)
    1. Snowboarding--Juvenile literature. I. Title.

GV857.S57W558 2012
796.939--dc23
                                                    2012004033

Crabtree Publishing Company

Printed in the U.S.A./032012/CJ20120215

www.crabtreebooks.com   1-800-387-7650

Published in Canada
Crabtree Publishing
616 Welland Ave.
St. Catharines, Ontario
L2M 5V6

Published in the United States
Crabtree Publishing
PMB 59051
350 Fifth Avenue, 59th Floor
New York, New York 10118

Published in the United Kingdom
Crabtree Publishing
Maritime House
Basin Road North, Hove
BN41 1WR

Published in Australia
Crabtree Publishing
3 Charles Street
Coburg North
VIC 3058

Contents

What is snowboarding?

Snowboarding is an individual sport done outdoors. A **snowboarder** rides a piece of equipment called a **snowboard** down a snowy hill or mountain. Snowboarding is similar to surfing, skateboarding, and skiing. Many snowboarding moves are the same as surfing moves and snowboarders can do tricks like skateboarders.

Snowboarders can do many of the same tricks as skateboarders.

4

Snowboarders can pick a run based on their experience.

Snowboard runs

Snowboarders can ride at ski resorts, funparks, and in the backcountry. Ski resorts have **runs** where snowboarders can carve down the slopes. Runs are usually rated for level of difficulty. A green circle marks easy runs, a blue square is for moderate runs, and a black diamond is for difficult runs. Unlike easy and moderate runs, difficult runs are not **groomed**, or flattened and smoothed. Difficult runs may also have **moguls**, or large snow bumps.

Gearing up

Snowboarding is done outdoors, so snowboarders must be sure to stay warm and dry. A snowboarder wears a windproof jacket, snow pants, gloves, and boots, with silk, wool, or **microfiber** clothes underneath. A snowboarder must also wear a safety-approved helmet and goggles to protect the eyes.

On and off layers

Snowboarders wear comfortable clothing that allows them to move freely. They also dress in layers so they can add and remove pieces to warm up or cool down.

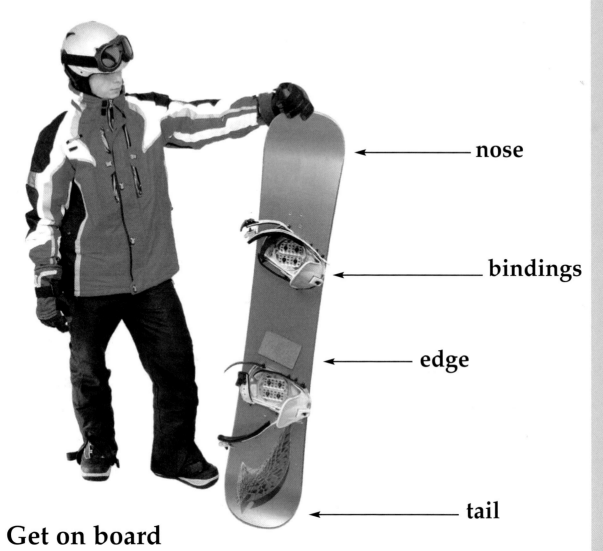

nose

bindings

edge

tail

Get on board

A snowboard is made of layers of wood, plastic, and **composite** materials. Composite materials are made of two or more materials. Steel strips along the edges help riders grip the snow. The front end of the snowboard is called the **nose**. The **tail** is the rear end of the snowboard. Straps called **bindings** are mounted to the board. Bindings fasten snowboarders' boots to the board.

Where to ride

Funparks have jumps and other **snow obstacles**, such as boxes and rails, for snowboarders to perform tricks on. Funparks may also have **half-pipes**, which are U-shaped ramps made out of snow where snowboarders do **aerial** tricks.

Into the wild

The backcountry is any steep, rocky, or remote area where snowboarders ride. These areas are not groomed like ski hills. Snowboarders in the backcountry need to watch for dangerous snow slides called **avalanches**.

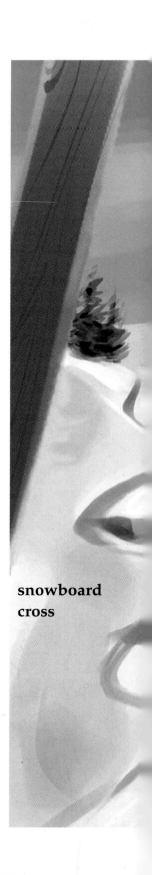

snowboard cross

A ski resort is an area in the mountains made for snowboarding, skiing, and other winter sports.

ski lift

slalom

half-pipe

inish line

finish line

Getting to the top

Before snowboarders go down the hill, they must go up. There are three ways to get to the top of the hill. One way is to climb up. Another way is to ride a bar shaped like a "T" called a **t-bar** to the top. T-bar lifts are often found at beginner slopes.

Snowboarders can ride a t-bar to get to the top of a hill.

These snowboarders are climbing up a hill.

Catching a lift

A third way is to take a chairlift to the top. With one foot free and the other strapped to the board, snowboarders move into position as the moving chair approaches. They grab the bar that holds the chair and sit down. They keep the board pointing straight ahead and lower the safety bar.

To get off the chair lift, snowboarders raise the safety bar. Once the board touches snow, they stand up. They place their free foot in the middle of the board and glide down an exit ramp.

Many ski resorts have chairlifts that snowboarders can use to get to the top of the hill.

Basics on the board

Just as people are right-handed or left-handed, snowboarders are **regular-footed** or **goofy-footed**. The names of these stances note which foot a snowboarder leads with on the board. Regular-footed boarders ride with their left foot at the front of the board. Goofy-footed riders ride with their right foot at the front.

goofy

regular

Regular or goofy?
To find out if you are regular-footed or goofy-footed, put a snowboard on the ground and try out each stance. One stance will feel more natural and comfortable than the other.

Finding balance

At first, balancing on a snowboard challenges most riders. Riders are bound to their boards, so they cannot move their feet to stop themselves from falling. They must learn to balance by leaning toward the front, or nose, of the board and the back, or tail, without falling over. They must also learn to rock their weight onto their toes and heels without taking a spill.

Snowboarders need good balance to stop themselves from falling.

Going downhill

Snowboarders rip down hills and mountains by **traversing**. Instead of pointing their boards straight toward the bottom of the hill, snowboarders angle their boards across the slope. That way, they can ride from left to right and right to left, zigzagging back and forth across the slope. Traversing helps riders slow down so they can control their speed.

Traversing is moving from one side of the slope to the other while going down the mountain.

Stop on the spot

When snowboarders want to stop, they nudge the nose of their boards uphill slightly. Then they rock their weight into their heels to dig the heelside edge of the board into the snow. This brings them to a quick stop.

Snowboarders turn and lean back to stop.

Rules of the Hill

- Ride with control, so you can always stop or avoid people and objects.
- Keep a safe distance between you and other riders on the hill.
- People ahead of you have the right-of-way. You must avoid them.
- Do not stop where you might block a run or cannot be seen from above.
- Use a **safety strap** to stop runaway boards.
- Take turns. Do not ride a snow obstacle while another rider is on it.

Board turning moves

Making smooth turns takes a lot of practice. Most riders also try to make **carved turns**, which take even more practice. Carved turns not only cut neat and tidy tracks in the snow, they also make a cool whooshing sound. Like all turns, carved turns are made on the toeside or heelside edge of the board.

When doing carved turns, the edge of the board leaves tracks in the snow.

First things first

To make carved turns, snowboarders must master **skidded turns** first. Looking in the direction they want to go, riders shift their weight into the front foot and rock onto the toeside or heelside edge of the board. Then they steer the board through the turn with the back leg.

To make carved turns, snowboarders must first master skidded turns.

Free-riding

Free-riding snowboarders ride down the mountain, and any other place they can find. Free-riders also ride groomed trails, carving turns from top to bottom, and traversing terrain in between.

Free-riding can be a lot of fun for experienced snowboarders.

Free-riders perform their tricks in any terrain they choose.

No limits

Free-riders may also drop in on the half-pipe, shred in and around trees, and hit the funpark. In this style of snowboarding, riders may also ride any and all terrains in the backcountry.

Freestyle

This style of snowboarding is the most like skateboarding. Freestyle snowboarders perform tricks, jumping and riding ramps, rails, tabletops, and other snow obstacles at a funpark. Snow obstacles are built for riders to get airborne and do tricks.

Snowboarders perform tricks on rails and other obstacles.

Ollies in the snow

Snowboarders do not need ramps or other obstacles to jump into the air. Snowboarders can do **ollies** just like skateboarders. They fly through the air with their snowboards stuck to their feet. Snowboarders can reach down with one hand and grab their boards. These tricks are called **side grabs**, **toe grabs**, or **tail grabs**, depending on which part is grabbed.

Snowboarders can do ollies to fly through the air, just like skateboarders.

In the half-pipe

Many resorts have a half-pipe—a U-shaped ramp made of snow. A half-pipe looks like a pipe that has been cut in half. It has a flat area in the middle with curved areas called **transitions** on each side. Each transition leads into a wall about 12 to 22 feet (3.6 to 6.7 meters) tall. The top edge of the wall is called the **lip**.

This is a good half-pipe for beginnners.
The walls are short and the slope is not very steep.

Snowboarders fly out of the ramp and perform tricks in the air.

Pump it up

Snowboarders drop into the half-pipe. They ride back and forth between the walls to build up enough speed to catch air, or fly above the walls. Once airborne, snowboarders can do a variety of tricks, such as grabs, spins, and flips. Top snowboarders can spin around three and a half times in midair before landing on the half-pipe.

Racing

Snowboarders can also take part in races. There are three main races on the hill: **parallel slalom**, **parallel giant slalom**, and **snowboard cross**. In parallel slalom, two riders go head-to-head. The riders race down the mountain side by side on identical courses. They twist and turn through gates. If riders miss one gate, they are disqualified. Parallel giant slalom is a similar race with gates that are farther apart, so riders go faster.

In parallel slalom, two riders race head-to-head.

Snowboard cross racers must have very good snowboarding skills.

Test of skill and nerve

Snowboard cross gets its name from motocross or dirt bike racing. Four to six racers zoom down the course of banked turns, bumps, and jumps at the same time. The varied course puts riders' boarding skills to the test—as well as their nerves. Riders go very fast and they often crash into one another. The rider who crosses the finish line first wins.

Competitions

Snowparks and resorts hold competitions for snowboarders of all levels, from beginner to pro. Top snowboarders also compete in the Olympics, X Games, and World Cup. Competitions at the Olympics include the snowboard cross, slalom, half-pipe, and slopestyle events. Unlike races in which the fastest rider wins, half-pipe and slopestyle contests have judges who award points.

Snowparks and resorts hold competitions for snowboarders of all levels.

A snowboarder rides the rail in a slopestyle competition.

Slopestyles

In slopestyle contests, individual riders complete a course of large jumps, rails, and varied terrain. Riders must flow smoothly from one obstacle to the next. Judges give them points just like in half-pipe events.

In the eyes of the judges

In half-pipe contests, riders perform **runs** of a number of aerial jumps and tricks. Judges give riders points for style, level of difficulty, landing cleanly, and amplitude. **Amplitude** is the height riders reach in the air as they do a trick. Riders do two runs. The scores of their runs are added. The rider with the highest total score wins.

Stars that rip

No snowboarder rules the half-pipe like Shaun White. Shaun started snowboarding when he was six years old. He learned the moves from his older brother Jesse. By the end of his first day on the hill, Shaun was going faster and jumping higher than his brother. Shaun won gold medals in the half-pipe at both the 2006 and 2010 Olympics. Shaun is also a champion skateboarder.

Shaun White has also invented tricks, such as the Double McTwist 1260—a double flip with three and a half spins.

Hannah Teter was the World Junior Half-pipe Champion at age 15.

Hannah Teter catches big air

Hannah Teter hopped on a snowboard for the first time when she was eight. She entered her first contest when she was 11, and was the only girl entered in her age group. It wasn't long before she began winning competitions. Hannah's wins include Olympic gold at the 2006 Games and silver at the 2010 Games in the half-pipe.

Carve it!

Hop on your board and carve your way down the hill. Snowboarding is a great sport for fun and fitness. Boarders get a lot of exercise carving down mountains and riding around snowparks. Snowboarding also helps develop balance and coordination. You need to stay steady on a moving board and move your body into different positions to do tricks—all without moving your feet.

The scene

Resorts and funparks usually welcome young riders. Many offer lessons to help kids learn snowboarding skills and encourage kids to snowboard for the fun of it.

Snowboarding helps develop balance and coordination.

You can find many new friends at snowparks.

Get out and have fun snowboarding!

Learning the basics first is important.

Glossary

Note: Boldfaced words that are defined in the text may not appear in the glossary.

aerial High in the air

bindings The straps that fasten a rider's boot to the snowboard

composite Something made of two or more materials

goofy-footed Riding with the right foot at the front of the board

groomed Smoothed and flattened snow at ski resorts

half-pipes U-shaped ramps made of snow that snowboarders perform aerial tricks in

microfiber A soft polyester fiber that can be used to make fabrics that are windproof and breathable.

moguls Large snow bumps

nose The front end of a snowboard

regular-footed Riding with the left foot at the front of the board

runs A downhill course that snowboarders ride from the top of the hill to the bottom; Also, a rider's turn or performance in half-pipe and slopestyle events

safety strap A strap that prevents a snowboard from taking off down the hill

snow obstacles Boxes, rails, and other obstacles snowboarders ride and perform tricks on

tail The back end of a snowboard

transitions Curved areas in a half-pipe that lead from the flat area into the walls

traversing Angling a snowboard across the slope of a hill to zigzag down the hill

Index